I0453496

THE *Art* OF BICYCLE RIDING

THE *Art* OF BICYCLE RIDING

JOSEPH MOCTEZUMA

"Your story is our priority"

LitPrime Solutions
21250 Hawthorne Blvd
Suite 500, Torrance, CA 90503
www.litprime.com
Phone: 1-800-981-9893

© 2022 Joseph Moctezuma. All rights reserved.

No part of this book may be reproduced, stored in a retrieval system, or transmitted by any means without the written permission of the author.

Published by LitPrime Solutions   10/27/2022

ISBN: 979-8-88703-079-1(sc)
ISBN: 979-8-88703-080-7(e)

Library of Congress Control Number: 2022919328

Any people depicted in stock imagery provided by iStock are models, and such images are being used for illustrative purposes only.

Certain stock imagery © iStock.

Because of the dynamic nature of the Internet, any web addresses or links contained in this book may have changed since publication and may no longer be valid. The views expressed in this work are solely those of the author and do not necessarily reflect the views of the publisher, and the publisher hereby disclaims any responsibility for them.

CONTENTS

L.A. IS THE PLACE

THE TRAVELING EDUCATOR

THE PHILOSOPHER

He wasn't good looking, and appears and disappears in a crowd without notice, yet his soft spoken voice captured the attention of sophisticated listeners in the area.

Of small stature but of incredible processed critical thinking

He was well educated; a Master in Education and a knack for writing, a skill that not many ordinary people have

He lived in one of the biggest metropolitan areas in the U. S. A. : Los Angeles, a city of dreams and decadence, of exuberant indulgence, of great achievements such as the air plane industry, the movie industry and computer industries. All of these made Los Angeles and California a prize to win for entrepreneurs and dreams from all over the globe

Young people of all walks of life came to play the rulette of fortune, with good looks, great ideas to captured that fleeing moment of glory or defeat,

Los Angeles is a constant moving jungle of concrete and steel,. The people who ride at 90 miles per hour also had a heart of steel and a concrete deterlmination to win at all cost

There was an underlying arrogance about their posture and outlook in life

My philosopher friend was humble in contrast and wanted to

prescribe a better behavior that would be the crown of this new
Angelino's civilization
When in his lecture to attentive listeners crowd he
would address them in a mosaic style of thought: Listen all of you
the wisdom of ages:

Justine like to ride bikes, ever since he was 9 years old, his Dad
bought him a bike and he went everywhere with it

He rode uphill, down hill and went to the market, He

THE BICYCLE CHRONICLES

life islike riding a bicycle, you always have to push forward or you will fall. By going forward, you balanced your weight on everything

Your weight is what keeps your position in this world

Some are so heavy weight that they cannot sustain their position in life. Is even heavy for them to ride a bike

They will bend the wheels that turns them around

Others are very light weight, they move with subtle speed and keep themselves in a very balanced flow

All things have a sense of weight, water is the weight of the universe!

Sustaining your weight against gravity before you fall is the trick of everyday living

A balanced life is just like riding a bike, all your weight has to be against gravity

Going against gravity gives you a certain freedom, with every step you make, you declared you are free from the fall. With every push you do on the bike, you get a sense of independence from the ground, from the earth that binds you,

The wind blows on your face, like th spirit blows in the crevices of your mind, making you wonder of things to come

You have to believe first that you escape in freedom by riding the bike

You have to believe in yourself that you can do it; that you can lift yourself oJf the ground with out falling

The world will make sense if you can liberate yourself out of something

Once he finished, he laid down his notebook and humbly thank the confused audience that applauded as a courtesy his daring display of philosophical thought >

There was no place for sophisticated thought in a place like L.A. where transactional endeavors and language of cash, finance and expense cars were the soup of the day
The only one that applauded with a sincere heart was an attorney that dwell in spiritualism and had a liking to his thinking and person

When I asked him (the philospher) about her he started saying in a low voice the following ;

WEIGHT

The first time I saw her, she placed a weight on me to see how much I value, and balance my life with vision of me.

Her career was coming to a closed, an attorney that made three or four million in her hey day of cases. Now she was doing the light side of an attorney life; trust and will and testament, one or two cases of divorce and labor suits etc.

She saw me with interest, coming from a different

background and culture, dark versus white, but she pu(t a little bit of weight in my life by training me and ordaining me in becoming a minister. she had a business in mind; weddings because assumed the pleasure of marrying people, but she left me the couples that could only speak Spanish.

We were called the "traveling ministerJ because we go to the site where the couple wanted to get marry: lobbies of hotel, parks or homes.

We married over 300 couples in our brief enterprise

Not a lot of money we made, but had our fun more so than profit

She bestowed the honor of calling me by the title "Reverent" which to me at the time, had a double meaning : a minister or a person who returns, after death as a ghost

She always thought that I had an Ancient spirit or old spirit, one that come again and again to life with many life experiences on his belt,

It always remind me of an animal that returns again and again to the water source of pond or lake to quench its thirst after roaming the savannahs of time and space.

She did have other interests like Astrology, reading palms and mystics. Her famous mystic was the Trappist monk, Thomas Merton, she always told me she wanted to write a book on Him, but her writing has a legal style that made it less friendlier to read

The weight that she installed in me was to appraised myself in time of change; Hollywood started to desconstruct itself; heaven being perfect, was not what we, our starving souls need, the starving soul of Merton look else where but in Christianity, seeking in the easts, Budha and the understanding of why we don't have to be save, for the simple reason that we do not want to be save,

The Hollywood 's standard gold for success, the "Oscars' were forever change in the "93" Oscars awards, where desperately seeking for Nostalgia, they had it in a train Station where everyone leaves town and no one ever takes responsabiity

We forsake heaven and perfection and did not want to be saved.

She was that type of spirit, rebellious, roarke, uncompromising, probably that was the reason she like Merton and his always waiting at the train station for the next train to the east,

Weight Second Part

Weight sustain us in reality, once we cannot accept reality, we slowly lift us up like a ballon, leaving totally our sense of what is solid and losinng our grasp of the earth, we are no longer in solid grownd

We losed our sense of being as we flow into an unconscious sky

It is for some people that give us weight that we sustain ourselves grounded. upon this earth

L.A. IS
THE PLACE

INCORRUPTIBLE

we cover ourselves with metal.
we hide our fleshy nature behind a shell of metal and vinyl;
so we don't have to smile to no one.
so that we don't have to speak to no one.
we become faces of glass and smiles of chrome.
our eyes only enlightens the outside, no longer do we take the
world inside.
we don't show emotions, only a frame of chrome as our smile and
in cold steel rods\our body becomes. no more the body electra
but the body combustion. we pretend that all is ilusion outside,
even the right signal of others and the only right away is us.

we ride on rubber wheels not going anywhere, moving everywhere
even though we all ready made predetermined roads
and established ways of concrete made blvds which do not lead
nowhere.
we are aisolated and find no destination to our pilgrimage of glass,
metal and concrete.

we have fashioned an incorruptible body for ourselves. one that
is preserve without emotions like a mummie.
in the old times an incorruptible body came with myrrh,

FRANCIDSENSE and aloe and Gold, the only metal that does not corruted.

it was a resurrected body of glory, one perserved for all times. carries a resemblance of immortality like an egipytian tomb inside a pyramide body of time.

it piggback its dreams of imortality in the quest of an incorruptible body through out the ages. because incorruptible ties to holiness, resurrection, immortality, salvation through the embalming with oil and myrrh..

Now our resurrected body is made of stainless steel. a body that is incorruptible and does not corrupt.

a body that moves you to all places. goes to all places, and protect you from the hard crashes of life.

eventhough we die to all our human emotions y human locomotion, we are resurrected with a SUV chevy Blazer in a neon heaven of speed and lights. we are not in one place anymore, we rolled in our highway to heaven entombed in our sarcafagus of metal looking always dead inside.

Living in Los Angeles I was brought up on tv and movies, ever since I was a child I always had an alternative reality, by seeing too much TV or movies; TV and Hollywood provided that alterantaive reality to kids of all ages, that is why Star Wars and Avengers become more real to us The world had a poor reality, but our imagination was unlimited and boundless. The Imagination of our minds is greater than the reality we live outside

There was a disonance of what the greater expectations we had for that celluloid alternative reality and our limited poor reality that we lived Sooner or later that disonance was going to make us bitter and disappointed in our hearts and mind where we could not accept anything less that the glamour of the stardust Hollywood reality

We are a generation of dreamers brooding with dissapoinment in Los Angeles, loading the outside world, encapsulating in a world of dreames like bubbles floating in empty space

THE TRANSITIONAL CULTURE

The American culture may be defined as "Transitional Culture"

It is heartfeld American to use a culture up to its utility or its opportunistic use of the value it has.

When the mother of invention: the need to make money through invention imposed upon society a new culture and we as a society adapt to it like wearing a different clothing for the new day.

The amazing ease to which we adapt as a society to a new culture is uniquely American, making it unique in comparison to other world cultures which adapt a culture for the long run.

The American society does not accept culture as an absolute, rather something transitional and temporal until the next invention, with the use of technology as a saving grace.

CULTURE AS AN IDENTITY

Other societies adopt a culture as an identity, a culture that will be worn for a thousand years. A culture that is identify with every single individual

Justine was ready for his second lecture in the
LightHouse of Knowledge, located in Anaheim
Early he backback all his papers to be early so he could set up
everything he needed

This time it was a motivational lecture with a positive point of view
It was formulated like the tenth commanments,
exept this time was seven principles of life;

Ladies and gentlemen, Mr Justine Buscary:

THE FLOW

How do become constant energy?

In order to become constant energy and regain the energy you have lost it is necessary to do these steps:

1) LOSE YOURSELF: the denial of yourselt is the first step in Budhisim and in Christianity: Jesus said : "Deny yourselt carry your cross and follow me". Buddha required for you to destroy the house of the ego, the self interest and the self agenda that you have in all things. let all things be free of yourself and you se yourself in all things

2) BE IN SYNCRON/CITY: Be In tune with the universe in accordance with your own steps. Be in God's rate of speed. You can ask yourself what is the rythenm that God runs in my life? A man that lives by the river, supplied himself with all the energy carry by the riverand he becomes famous by his vitality and rhythm going withs the rhythm of all things in motion. He let his heart lose in the river's current and he runs with the same speed as the speed and rhythm of the universe. ;be One with the all.

3) BE YOURSELF A FLOW: be yourself a river! a river runs

through you Let all things flow through you. Conceive your mind, body and soul as a the surface of a sea and see how peaceful and serene you can make it.

4) NO RESISTENCE : do not resist evil or tragedy or pain or suffering, because you utilized them to let go of things, to purify yourselt and obtain the energy to transcend your own self and life. Once you are trapped into a cage, you already been liberated because you have transcended your condition when there is no way out.

5) AWARENESS: to be aware is to be conscious and to be conscious is to see not outside but go inside, towards the inside. It is an inward vision of you and of the world. There are three types of mind in awareness: Empty mind, Open Mind and Close mind: the closed mind becomes a jail or imprisonment for those who Jive their lives inside their problems. It becomes an obsession. An open mind is when you live outside the things and problems of life. You do not see yourself in the things you have seen or obtained but you are always open to see the sun. in this open mind you are at rest. It becomes a sabbatical style of rest: you open space to posses, have and act. You open time to have quality time and to live within the moment. You open a Bliss for yourself; a place and a state that you find for you. Empty mind is that which you empty your mind of all things to find peace, rest and renewal and restoration of self: it is like cleaning house and the mind cleanses. A purification by which it brings the four P's : power, peac, protection, and purification. thus empty yourself and be not a stumbling block to yourself therefore the results of awareness is to be open, to be present, to be conscious and to be one with all.

6 MINDFULLNESS: Brings fulfillment, wholeness and completeness. It is the attention of the intimate of your self and the enclosure of self. You see yourself in things that you have perceived. It is a higher form of awareness because it focus is on 1/umination and control and everything has a reflection in you! You focus in attentive seeing and you have the energy to Meditate and the result will be Peace, the bliss within you. You focus and attentive seeing, you use the energy to Contemplate and as a result you will obtain Presence. You focus on attentive seeing and you wil have the energy to Reflect and as a result you will have the Four P's: Purification, Power, Protection and Peace. You focus and attentively see, then you have the energy for Prayer then you fill have the Flower of Consciouse Awareness which means you can participate with the Divi nel Interprete the Diving in human terms for the need of the needy and Intergrate body and mind I the interior and the exterior to be one and to be born again of Spirit. Amen

7) ENERGY REGAINED.: Energy is the vitality of Being it is a complementary fulfillment of wha a ab eing is to itself by knowing of itself and completely to itself.

Joseph Moctezuma Rivera Dec 5,   2016

Justine got sick, a strange illness that immobilized the body little by lit/le weakening the muscles of the body to become a prison for Justine

Joseph was her friend that help her with her everyday life chores : by going to the market, taking care of the house maintenance while Justine emersed little by little int the subconscious quiet state of mind where the Thetha brain electric level spring out in a creative and innovated manner, to spring new ideas out of her mind;

"do you want vegan burgers for lunch? Asked joseph to Justine. No thanks, I will stay with my yogurt abd cracjkers, replied Justine, positioning herself in a Yoga posture and her mind set in the Beta State,

Let's go and eat lunch in the garden. She commented after I bring the grocery from the store Yes let's do that, Justine remark and see how beautiful flowers Spring brought

THE GARDEN'S TREE

I had a garden in my backyard. Where I used to plant and nourish all types of flowers. In the middle of the garden there was a tree that my friend gave me.

When I planted it the tree gr w in size and gave fruits in abundance

When I show my friend the tree how it grew in my garden, he started to describe it in a different way and form to delineated a transcendental reality

Corne on, justine, do not tell me that that tree has magical powers? It does Joseph, if ;you believe that it does., reality, our own reality is some how link to your believe How is that? I said to him, that thru a tree we can ascertained transcendental truth of our own reality, tangible and material?

You see, Joseph, those birds corning to land in the tree? Just imagine that they are minds, wanting to; find a place on those branches. The mind is a free bird that somehow wants to land find in those branches a place and it becomes a mind because of its position in the branches, once the bird change branches and its position on the tree, the mind changes. the mind is bird on the tree, each bird is a mind and the tree is like our bodies and the branches are the blood of the flowing spirit in us

The position of the bird on the tree is a state of mind Now the mind is trapped out of its own will because it eats of the fruit that the tree gives, once one eats of the fruit, a new reality is given to us in us and outside of us. We can stay in that reality forever, for there is no reality in space and in time, or out there in the universe, only the one that we bestowed upon us after eating the fruit,

Justine, I think you are on something or you took a certain drug that make you see too a simple tree a whole new reality of life and of the universe. How do you come up with that type of thinking?

Joseph, Joseph, reality is created.! The universe is based on believe, there is no such thing as matter. By itself! All things are interconnected and replaceable once you dicover or it reveal to you a new reality, a new mind set, a new way to understadn life

How about time? Justine

The mind is just time or time is mind joseph Stop there Justine, lets get a coffee and enjoy thi beautiful California weather.

Justine continue talking about the mind this way:

"I once read Jose Silva's book: "the Silva method of Mind Control "and it taught me quite a hit about hrians waves and how they are described as : Alpha, Beta, Theta, Delta and so on, hut what was so intriguing to me that we can bend reality by changing our mindset or by meditaion
Can we change our future and bend our reality by switching those brain waves thru simple meditations techniques? Said Joseph
Yes, Joseph, said Justine, the mind is tied in to a universe that becomes, desires to be and belong

The mind can see the past, change the future by desiring the present to be > ousr present is sthe key and our mind presence as a crystal ball, can move the past and change the future by desiring the present tense of our mind
Wow!, that is too heavy for me.
There are different types of mind; and I am going to describe to you Now,

The Gesthalic Mind:

this mind has the ability to go beyond the parts in existence and see things as a whole ; I called it Panoramic world view of things. Enviromentalists would define it as "think globally, but act locally". Contrary to this mind is the reductional mind that can only see the parts, but not the whole., can see the tree but not the forest.

The Vicarious Mind

This mind has the ability to emptying itself or dissolving itself into the object with the subject : YOU ARE THE NUMBER: you are what you eat, you are what you do. You are what you think

The Icarius Mind

Has the ability of sizing the problem in relation to the size TO us. With relative size to us a matter of importance ITS a matter of size.

Some people make things big because of their fear and likewise make it small due to their ignorance,

The numeric Mind

Has the ability to look only at the transaction, never anything else,. it only works with a complete set, so to divide, add or multiply. To make things whole again in a numeric way. To make things equal without persuing justice.

Invent imaginary numbers so there would be a solution.

Yet the numeric mind never goes beyond completeness. Never see a world outside quantity Never measure anything until it invents a two after the one

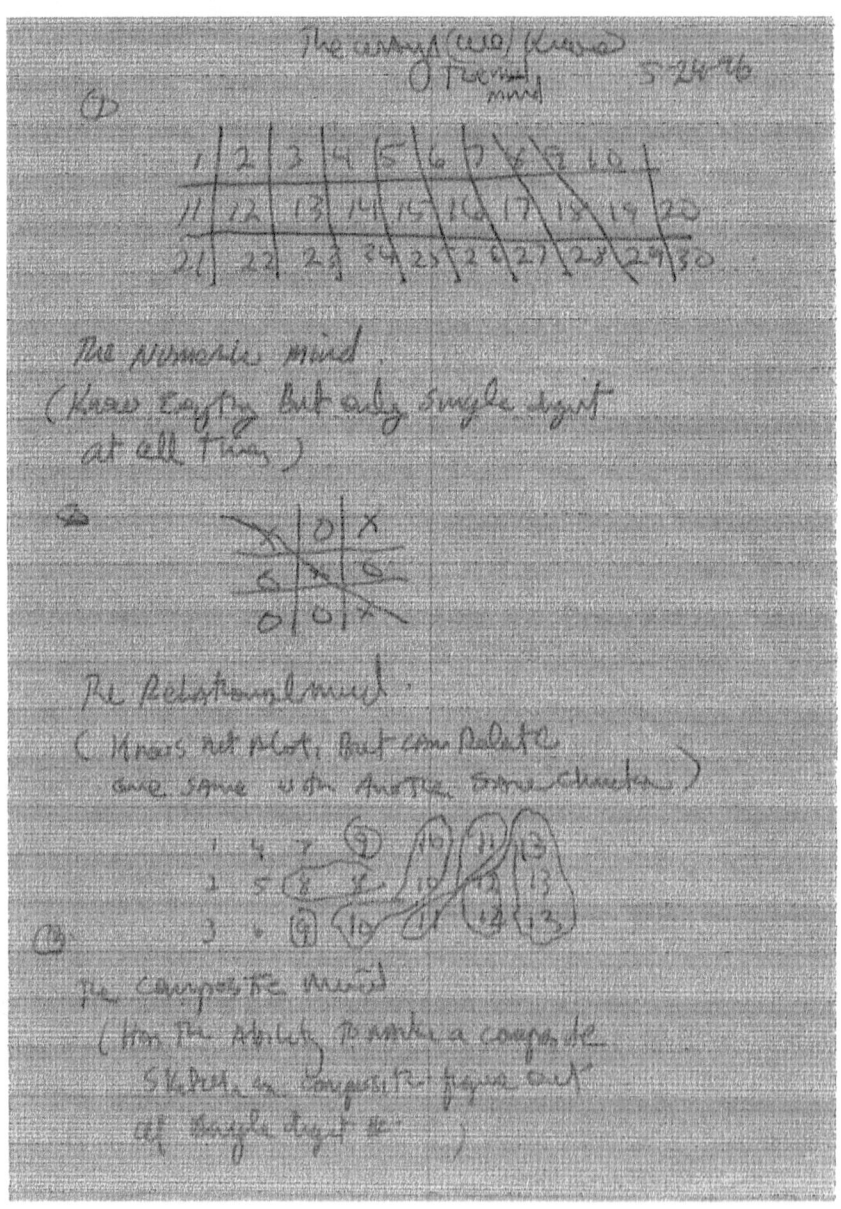

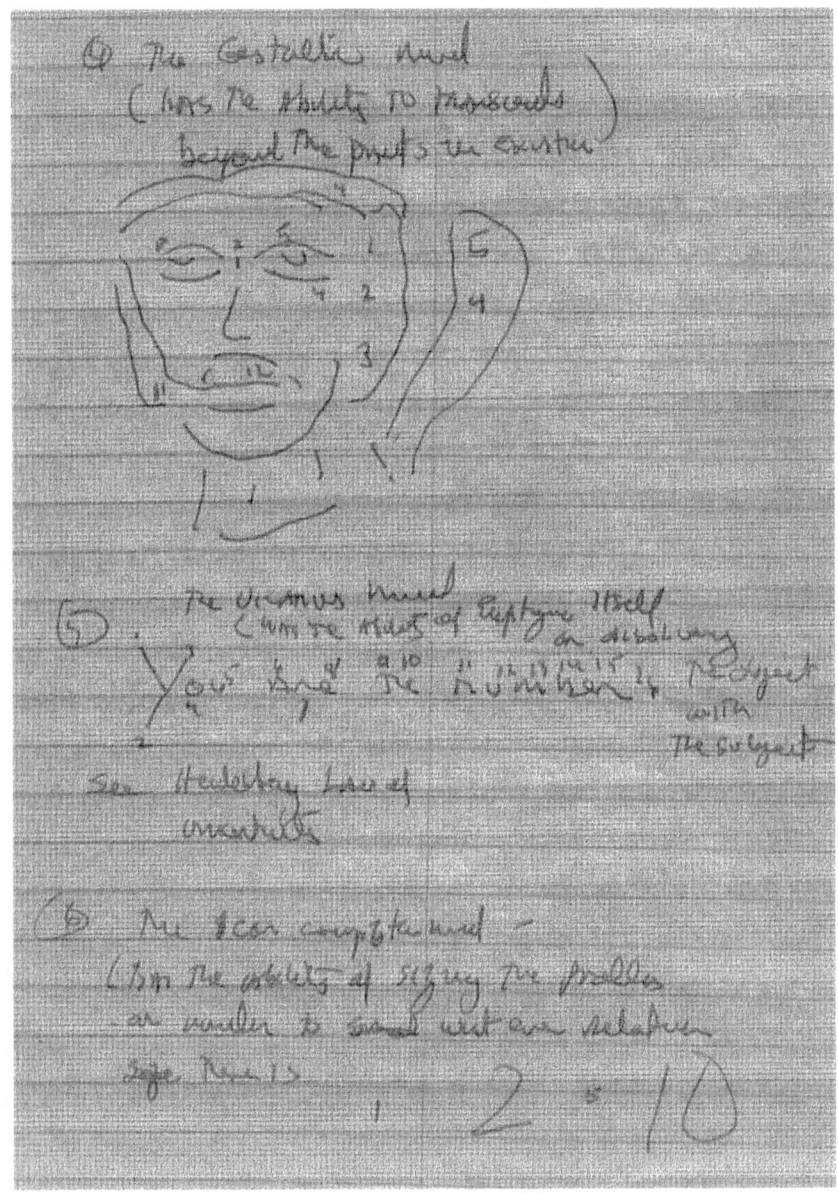

BRAIN'S ALGORITHMS

It is amazing how the brain or mind can associate words and concepts identifying similar ideas and similar concepts in a cascade of similarity. similar to an algorithms working with association of words and concepts

Also the mind work with not only words and concepts, but with similar theories and happenings which allows the mind to have faith and convictions of the reality it lives or experience
The mind rejects the words or concepts that are not similar, the same way it rejects the theories or happenings that are not similar to its own faith or reality
By this mental process we bring order to chaos and stability to a reality that becomes familiar and reject all estrangement from a universe that is chaotic and insane in logic and reason

Justine, our friend the philosopher, had another lecture announced for this Friday evening. Not a lot of people came, some curious to meet a true philospher, an others that did like his previous lecture on Weight

This lecture was on Patterns, and as usual he stand on a podium and address his audience in this form:

PATTERNS

There are two elemental rules in the universe that applies like gravity : one is the pattern that exists in all things material and inmaterial in the world; the second is the rhythm of things and of God's that flow with everything

Patterns are everywhere and it make everything repites itself in constant copies of the previous pattern

By repiting itself I it sustain life and design I from protein to stars, without a pattern there would not be a design for matter, it would be a constant flux I chaos with no end at sight or beginning for that matter

Bouscary was observing the symbols engraved in this ancient astrolabe found in a sunken ship near the sea of Cortez

She was a poet, describing the meaning within a poem. she was a decoder of languages, of hidden symbols and translation

For her

She am Hi & she of Fu Soul

FORMULA FOR SUCCESS

There is a pattern for everything, the formula for success starts with finding the pattern for anything that you want, desire or set goal to.

Passion has a pattern. Your passion has a particular pattern; it requires that you must follow you heart in life, keep you heart in you hand and it will guide you through life like a JPS giving you directions and avoiding deters.

The American Dream had a formula : you go to school, you graduate, you find a good job, you work hard, you married, buy a home, have kids and retired with a nice pension for your latter years. There was nothing stopping for anyone to achieved success by following this formula

Then things changed and it was not that easy anymore.

The formula for success for this era of uncertainty and diminishing returns is to know yourself and find the skills and talents that you can transfer with to another field and be able to adapt them to that particular field of enterprise

The transferable skills and talents are essential for economic survival.

The second thing is to be adaptable to new circumstances by learning new things and unlearning old knowledge on things on a daily basis. learn, unlearned and learn again in the same day. Things do not retain permanency anymore: the one faithful in your day, will be unfaithful the very next day.

And the ability to adapt to these new demands required flexibility of mind and body

New era is upon us and old things and rules and established customs have disappeared.

Learn to be new always in this new age. Nothing old shall be accepted.

Renew yourself.

How does a philosopher make an earning? That was one persistent question that the audience asked of Justine

He mentioned very quietly that he was an educator, a traveling educator AND TOLD THE FOLLOWING STORY ABOUT HIM

THE
TRAVELING
EDUCATOR

When Justine was 14 years old, his cousin took him to the movies, where he saw, "To Sir With Love". a moive about a black teacher, teaching on the poor side of London, and the trials and tribulations of teaching some rag tag raggedy group of students.

Before the movie was over, Justine knew what he wanted to be: a teacher bringing light of knowledge to the forsaken kids, left stranded on the road to success.

THE TRAVELING EDUCATOR

I always though that a teacher has always a classroom A place that he can called home in so many ways Than one.

In my twenty years of being outside and looking in, of being a "traveling educator " being send to one high school to another, having no desk or chair, but willing to teach, to eduate and console the many with their inability to learn or learning disorder

I was there for anyone who could listern and be willing to take a chance on me, a nt typical teacher and a physical aspect of a gardener or a parking attentant

Short, stucky and with a thick accent with a quiet voice that no one heard in a noisy classroom

I was there in presence and spirit, wiling to help, to serve and to be rewarded just by a smile of excitement from the student, with big widening eyes of Eureka because she found the answer.

Nothing was more rewarding than that expression of a young student, surprising his mind to see the world in a different way.

I was born to be in that actualized moment of enlightment I was a traveling educator moving from one school to another, from one district to another in an endless circle of finding a place called home

For miles and miles I road the lonely streets, hightways and by ways seeking for alerted minds and an attention spand of more than 45 minutes to made it possible that birth of the mind to see a new world, dimension or reality that would form his or her future by building a vision of his or her wants and desires,

It's a learning processs that takes places not in a physical department or place, but in the mind in architectonically building the Eiffel tower of the mint/

AUTISTIC CREATIVE WORLD

You asked yourself this question : can a person full of shortcoming and limited in his behavior can become creative and even successful in his enterprise or business activity?

This strange question came about when I was working for a school district at Orange County 1 1 working with Autistic students I on a one on one basis or as a group I that is went I started to realized how talented and creative these students are.

Even though my master degree was obtained to work in education field I I did not intended to work in the Special Education field I but in order to get in the district I you start helping out the Special Educational Students of the School or ESL -English as a second language students which because of their disadvantage of not knowing English. Yet to be an ESL teacher was my first preference I although the school was in desperate need to hiring a behavioral specialist for these students. I took some tests and I became a behavioral assistant

The first impression I received after meeting them I was they live in a bubble world all of their own. they are excluded from mainstreaming in high school 1 yet they are given differential education treatment as well as special classes

I took them or guide them to Art Class ad I was very much impressed by their creative skills and talent I no where I seen such fresh approach to vision and pesrspective as they explore in their painting

THE SAMARITAN MAN

It happened in June 10, 2021 when I was buying water from the water store., I bought an extra 5 gallon bottle and the attendant put it in my car to take it to my car.

As I was bringing it down with difficulty, an old lady with her long white hair, with a grannie outfit, gentle approach me and ask me if I need it help,

I was strucked by her insistence, "let help you, please let me help II she said with a willingness of an angel, with caring and gentleness she insisted again that I have gave in to her request and she hold my cart as I brought it down, and she grap the heavier bottle of water as she was carrying something very light and not heavy. I did not know what to say and what to make of this situation

All I could understand that God wants to help me with my burden and my yoke will become so light that an old lady, much older than me, can and is willing to carry as feather the living waters of life

For I have to carry the living water of life to make fruitful all things I encounter on my path and bring the thirsty the living water of life. to bring the desert life would of today and quench its thirst

Once the water bottles were inside the trunk of my car

She in reverence made the sign of the cross, and I as I exalted her in front of her company

She told me she was from Castle by the sea in Italy and that she wasCatholic, I declare that I was too, and she inquired where can one worship here, being that she was a newcomer in town, I told her there was two catholic churches I mentioned and gave her directions

She left and I was amazed of how an old lady with a pure heart can transformed you and give to you the message from God: 'let mehelp you, please let me help you....

By believing, You own the Knowledge

justine third philosophical lecture came in early spring, just before Summer

His lecture was on Belief, a very intangible subject, comparing to his other lectures on science or the uni•verse.

His claim that the world has to have a belief foundation in order to functional, be operational, and productive was unique and weird, but he started with these words :

By believing, you own the knowledge

THE FOUNDATION OF BELIEF

All things were laid and foundation placed before anything happened in the universe

This is the foundation of belief I that things were made so you can claim your right of doing them. You cannot do anything in this world that was not meant for your to do it. nothing would be shown if it is not for you to see it

You see it because it is already established to be shown. you can do it because it has been already established for you to do it I otherwise nothing would be given to you

Believe is the predisposition of things to give valediction to all the happenings that will happens next

The universe is vindicated by your belief. it only takes for you to believe in things seen and unseen. Prove the universe right by your belief.

OWN THE KNOWLEDGE

1) Believe
   All things have been given to you already

2) Ownership- own the situation, the limitations and the oppurtunity!

3: Be Self Confident: YOU CAN DO IT

4; Knowlegde is power : or power is knowing

5:Things do not come by themselves: you must make things work

6. Be one with everything

7. Be open

8. Be present

9. Be joyful, happy and Blessed and obtain Bliss

10. Be Truthful

11. Be Known

12 be yourself

13. Be real

OWN THE KNOWLEDGE

This is my first effort to give wisdom to whom wants to learn a more positive path in life with the following few principles for his or her empowerment and success

1. BELIEVE!
Nothing can be done unles you believe, in yourself, in others and in the creation of the world
a. all things been given to you already
Believe is the afirmation that is all things created are true.
The affirmation, the conviction and the confidence to believe that all things are true
Believe is seeing, believe is vision, believe is seeing beyond yourself
Believe is also belonging, being a part of something
Believe is also becoming, you do not become or belong until you grow in yourself
You cannot go places and become someone else until you believe and grow and become
Believe there is a tomorrow, you become that tomorrow, believe in the stars, you become that star. Believe is just a transportation of your being to become something or someone your would like to he,
Believe is the nature of God in us, just like our God that see what

is not there, it has never been there and He makes it possible and has the power of believe to become real, without ever been there That is the magic of the heavens above; that they make it all possible for everything on the Earth, Heaven is married to the earth with possibilities, and the earth is married to heaven because of belief

BELIEVE, BELONG, BECOME No matter how impossible it is, amen

Belong is the universal yearning for the spirit to belong to a greater reality, to a greater existence than himself
It is the type of knowledge that is own by the heart

We own it because it is an essential ingredient for our happiness, Belonging is to recognize you are a part of something, greater than yourself,
That you are only a part of a world of posssihilities You are part of a universe. and the universe won't work without you, like a machine won't work if one of its part is missing. That is why it is so vital to save every little piece of moment in time, of every grump that falls from the table is pick up
The Parable of the loaves and fishes emphasizes that message almost at the end, where Jesus command his diciples to pick up all the pieces of food left and "do not leave a single grump left without picking it up"

Nothing is lost in this world, for God has accountability for every one that is lost
The Parable of the lost sheep, the Lost Coin, the Prodigal lost son. All these parable addresses the same subject. That we belong to our flock, or fold and once lost, Heaven and Earth will move to find us and be accounted for in the Eyes of God

It is vital for us to live and to know these things and once we know we BECOME WHAT WE ALWAYS Were made to BE. Becoming is a growth of the Spirit. For everything that is born, grows with the Word, the Spirit and Will of God,
Own the knowledge, you already become what you always going to be in heaven on earth and in your heart.

RHYTHM

God has a rhythm that we all must follow the flow with
If you are not synchronizing with the rhythm of God, you are not
synchronizing withs thee rhythm of everyday life.
When you play basketball you are not only in sync with your
steps, butalso in sync with everybody else in the team. you keep
yourself flowing with the speed and rhythm of the rest of the
team you don't let go of it
If you are dancing, you do not let go of your partner
You go with the rhythm of the music, the music dictate patterns
for your steps
You lead and she follows, you stop and she fall on top of you,
because you cannot stop and the music will never stop
Nor the basketball game will never end,

MIND DIRECTIONS

MERITDOESNOTBRINGSUCCESS

Success does not come by merit of your efforts! You can work all your life and never achieved success! Or wealth

WHA HAPPENS IS PARAMOJUNT!

It is not yoy either: it is not who or what your are that changes your life or wellbeing, it is rather what happens to you that changes your life, times and meaning or purpose. Your can say we are creature of circunstances or of destiny that plays a greater role in our lives,

PLACE IS IMPORTNANT

It is also that place is very important in our succes, it is where you placed yourself that opportunity arrives.

DESPOSITJON

It is also your actitude or desposition that opens up all alternatives tat you have in your hands!
It opens choices for success in your life
Be open with a good actitude and be albel to listen, to see and understand all alternative are at your reach!

YOU ARE THE LEVERAGE

Placed yourself outside the orbit and find a fixed point and you can move the whole world from your fixed point.
You are the leverage which moves worlds in the making

Fron a sinple fixed point of your being

YOU ARE THE BIGGEST DREAM

The biggest thing you own or have is your dream Therefore you cannot build a mountain bigger than you or your dream.
There is nothing bigger than you Vision o Dream! Think big, dream big, walk tall and ask for all or everything

THE PRESENT JS PRESENCE

We give up everything in the past to be one moment in the present because present is always better than the past.
We have losed a lot in the past to arrives in the present moment, All the generations of the past struggle with all their might so that you could be in the present moment of time,. This is how important is the present moment

Live for today and for the now.

OWN THE OPPORTUNITY

Own the knowledge that will bring you blessings in your life/ own the failure for it will bring your experience. Own the illness that make you stronger, Own your dream and ambition, tha will lead you to what is yours in others, in the world and in reality Claims what is yours in this life, for it will be given to you by angels and they will claim what your got from them
Ownership is the final step of success.

CREATE SPACE,

Create your space in life, not game in Beisball, footblla, basketball

or Soccer can be won if you do not create a space for a goal, basket, touchdown! We open space to live, to expand and to grow.
Create space and time is well used in your life and time
Create space for yourself, open yourself to new thngs, open yourself to new ambitions, ope, yourself so that the sky will be let in,

On top of the 13 floor of the hospital for mental disorders, a door open and a group of doctors in Pychology came in to see the patient that for 13 years he was left and abandoned by his family due to his insame behavior and strange talk that noone could understand "its Fridal the 13th, so this is a good time to bring the body out and take it to a Funeral homel
What was her name? said the another. Her name was Justine Bouscary, she was always talking crazy things in her mind. Nobody understood anything she said, and when she fell sick from Parkinson "s decease she was a prisoner in her own body
Didn"t she gave lectures?
No, it was all in her mind, she went around the garden talking to people about everything under the sun
She is now quiet and forever her mind is lose
A wonder/ul mind and great wisdom inside the. prison of her own body and forever dead to the world
Was there any loss to the world? No I do not think so, the world will never know the possible Truth That would have been, but that never was...

www.ingramcontent.com/pod-product-compliance
Lightning Source LLC
Chambersburg PA
CBHW020344130626
46549CB00003B/1277